Steps in My Shoes
The Life of a Foster Child

Ron Deming

STEPS
in My
SHOES
The Life of a Foster Child

Ron Deming

ISBN 978-0-692-86434-0 (print)

Dedicated
to all the
former, current, and future
foster youth
struggling to find their own place
in this world.

Acknowledgements

Some of my insights stem from research done by Elaine Aron, Ph.D. It was her research about highly sensitive people that helped me understand myself better. Thank you Pamelaanderson6 from Fiverr.com for professionally editing my book. Also, thanks to Alerrandre from Fiverr.com for the excellent work put into creating the book cover. This book would not have been possible without the help I received from numerous people throughout my life. I am most thankful to God who has helped me more than everyone else combined. This book would never have happened if He did not lay the importance of the message on my heart consistently for over a decade.

Contents

x

Author's Note

Moving from place to place, made me repress memories from past experiences in order to focus on adapting to my current situation. This totally screwed up my memory, so trying to recall descriptions and conversations would not have been possible unless I wanted to make it up and have it end up as fiction. Instead, I focused on the most important takeaways from each step in my life and provided insight to help readers put themselves in my shoes. The strategies and techniques I used in my life are not professional advice, so please seek a professional if you want in-depth help for your unique situation.

CHAPTER ONE
First Five Years

I went into the foster care system with my oldest biological sister because we were severely neglected. I did not learn the specifics, but it was bad enough to be covered on the news in Fort Wayne, Indiana. I went to my first foster home when I was between two and three years old. My sister who I went into foster care with is two years younger than I am, so this move did not affect her in the same way. Our first foster home was meant to be a temporary placement for my sister and I until we went back to our biological family or got adopted.

Being removed from my biological family had a negative impact on my behavior. I had built strong bonds with some members of my biological family, so losing them caused me great pain that manifested itself in the form of anger. One member of my biological family I had strong bonds with was my maternal grandfather. He would give me a lot of attention and I would get very upset anytime he left. The manner I expressed my anger about being separated from my family were not acceptable. This resulted in punishment for me; I was made to stand in the corner.

My biological sister and I moved into our first adoptive home about a year after entering the foster care system. Our parents had their rights terminated and this was a closed adoption, so there was no further contact with our biological family after leaving our first foster home. Our first adoptive parents were amazing people who had their own biological daughter who was older than I was. The anger I developed within the last year intensified further and I became violent towards both of my sisters. My first adoptive parents tried their best to help me control my anger, but it was too intense for them to handle without professional help. My first adoptive parents tried many different strategies to help me improve before they resorted to professional help.

One of the main ways my first adoptive parents tried to help me manage my behavior was to provide incentives for good behavior and charting the progress to a reward. The incentives did not work as intended because I was not interested in the rewards, so I saw no reason to improve my behavior. I was also discouraged when I saw how much progress my sisters had made toward their reward compared to me. My first adoptive parents also tried improving my behavior by putting me on timeouts and having me take out my anger on a pillow.

I sometimes threatened to run away when I got angry, so my first adoptive parents would pack up my clothes in brown paper bags and set them on the front porch so I could leave if I wanted. I would take the bags of clothes down to the end of the driveway and stop there because I did not know where to go. I stood by the mailbox and got embarrassed which fed my anger further, so it took a while for me to calm down. I would eventually take my bags of clothes back to the house when I realized there was nowhere to run away to and my anger subsided.

I have had people suggest my first adoptive parents wanted my sister and not me. I don't think they would have tried so many ways to help me improve if they were trying to get rid of me. Most loving parents would remove a kid from their home if their children were in physical danger and they could not fix the source. I grew up thinking I would never give up on my children no matter how badly they acted because I did not understand the situation from a parent's point of view. My first adoptive parents decided to have me admitted to Charter Beacon to see if the professionals there could help.

Charter Beacon was a behavioral health facility where staff attempted to help me manage my anger and other issues. The staff were not able to help me much because I did not form bonds of trust with them due to my reactive attachment disorder (RAD). Having RAD meant I was resistant to forming bonds with people and did not trust caretakers to provide for my needs due to the neglect I experienced. My RAD was possibly an adaptation mechanism to protect myself from the possibility of caretakers leaving me. The symptoms of my RAD probably gradually worsened after I was taken from my neglectful biological family, lived with multiple families, and was placed at a facility at a young age. These are all known causes of RAD, so it is not clear if one or a mixture of these factors caused it since the diagnosis is considered between uncommon and extremely rare.

Another characteristic that influenced my behavior was sensory processing sensitivity (SPS). SPS caused me to feel and think deeper than others who are not highly sensitive. It is apparent that anger I felt from my experiences was far worse than other angry children because RAD and SPS are both known to intensify feelings. The staff at Charter Beacon most likely struggled to help me manage the anger amplified by SPS and RAD because my mistrust interfered. They overcame these challenges enough to teach me that violence was not appropriate, no matter how angry I got. I don't know how the staff accomplished this, but I never had anger blackouts, which was when I became violent, after this point. The improvements I made at Charter Beacon were not enough for my first adoptive parents to let me continue staying with them.

I had all my belongings packed in the back of a car and was driven to my second foster home. I did not understand exactly what was going on because the lady driving me was very vague about our destination. I kept looking at my stuff then looking out the window watching the landscape go by. I arrived at my second foster home and that was when I got hit with the reality that this was my new home and I was now separated from my biological sister. I became so angry that I closed my eyes and crawled around the kitchen, banging my head into the cabinet doors. My second foster mom held me and calmly talked to me until I settled down.

My second foster mom tried a new strategy to help me control my behaviors and they worked better than the incentives. She gave me activities such as chores to keep me occupied so I would focus on those tasks instead of my negative feelings. One of the more successful techniques for improving my behavior was running when I got angry. My anger gave me extra energy for running and my anger would weaken as I got tired from running. Giving me the responsibility to feed my pet turtle with worms I found outside also helped me not to focus on my negative feelings.

I had three teenage foster sisters at my second foster family and I looked up to them as role models. My foster sisters had been through a lot over the years before coming to this foster home and were well-adjusted, so they were good examples for me. My foster sisters gave me attention and there was a bond we shared of having passed through similar circumstances, which helped me feel a sense of belonging. This was not meant to be a permanent placement, which was unfortunate because I had improved my behavior while I lived there. One of my foster sisters had a bigger influence on me because she talked to me the most and she inadvertently influenced me through her desire to never be adopted again. I wanted to do the same, so I could be like her even though I did not understand yet that her being a teenager made her situation different from mine.

CHAPTER TWO
Second Adoptive Home

My second adoptive mom had her hands full as a single mother with five children each with their own issues from traumatic pasts. My second adoptive mom worked as a physical therapist, so she could afford sending us to private school. She spent a lot of her time outside of work, dealing with our behavior problems with little to no progress to show for it. I had an older adoptive sister, two adoptive brothers from Texas, and one adoptive brother from Bulgaria. My two brothers from Texas were destructive, threw tantrums that required them to be restrained, and required a lot of our adoptive mom's attention.

I never stopped missing my oldest biological sister and for many years, would cry myself to sleep thinking about her. The only wish I ever had when blowing out candles for my birthdays was to see my sister again even though I knew how unlikely it was to happen. I was only able to visit with my biological sister a couple times after entering my second adoptive home at six years old. One scheduled outing was at a park where we had fun going down the slide together and the other was at a Nutcracker play. My second adoptive mom tried to set up more outings, but my first adoptive parents kept cancelling, so she stopped trying so I would not get my hopes up and be disappointed.

I attended a Catholic private school in Michigan City, Indiana while living with my second adoptive mom. One of my first memories at this school happened in first grade when I was told I needed to go back to kindergarten and I refused to go. The principal and janitor carried me to the kindergarten classroom with me fighting to get free the whole way. Moving back to kindergarten was a common consequence of foster care because kids lose an estimated four to six months of academic progress each time they are moved around. I was angry about being moved back to kindergarten because it was another example of not having control over my own life.

The deeper thinking and feeling I had from SPS helped me get into the heads of people and I used this to my advantage. I used this ability to manipulate people by accurately planning scenarios and conversations beforehand and twisting them to fit my selfish desires. I was too busy focusing on my selfish desires to notice how my actions were affecting the people around me. I felt that my suffering gave me an excuse to use people so I could make myself feel better and in control. I also felt that people owed me for all I had been through even though they had nothing to do with it.

One confusing and seemingly contradictory aspect of RAD is how I avoided making bonds with new people and yet was also clingy. It felt awkward yet natural when I would go from not caring if someone was my friend to trying to be around them as much as I could. This happened because I was protecting myself with apathy before the friendship started and protecting myself from the pain of losing the friendship by devoting a lot of attention to preserve the connection. I did not know how else to soothe my worries of potentially losing this new friendship even when it was apparent that I was probably smothering my new friend with attention. I eventually protected myself by finding an acceptable balance between emotionally distancing myself and strengthening the friendships I already had.

My grandmother at my second adoptive home helped me towards self-improvement even though her methods annoyed me because I thought she was just being mean. She would say things like "Poor trashcan Ronnie" when I complained about stupid stuff. I was trying to get other people to feel sorry for me and she did not put up with that nonsense when she was around. Later, I would repeat these sayings when I started feeling bad for myself. Internalizing these sayings helped me stop whining about my circumstances and putting that effort into further adapting to them instead. I figured out that I did not want the pity of those around me and found the inner strength to deal with challenges instead of using them for excuses to not accomplish my goals.

My intense enjoyment of a popular trading card game consumed my life when I became obsessed with collecting the cards. I stole my entire class' fieldtrip money out of the teacher's desk and spent all of it on these cards. I also used my lunch money to buy these cards and would have tried to steal them if they were not in a glass display. My obsession was so strong that my negative actions felt acceptable even though the cards were just pictures printed on cardboard. I lost my entire collection of trading cards when my second adoptive mom found out I stole the fieldtrip money.

My second adoptive mom would occasionally have a heart-to-heart talk with me to help me understand the negative impact of my behaviors. I had an overwhelming desire to make some self-improvements because of these talks, but the feeling faded when I realized I could not make the changes overnight. I eventually learned a process which helped me make permanent self-improvements after I accepted the fact that positive changes were going to take a lot of effort. My self-improvements were gradual changes that required a lot of determination and commitment. My obsession to continue making self-improvements over the years is one of the only times I have been thankful for how intense my obsessions can be.

The process I used to make long-term improvements started with deciding to become a better person because no one could make that decision for me. This part of the process was helped by the wonderful people I met in my life who I wanted to emulate. I saw how these selfless people had a fulfilling life and I wanted to be like them someday, so I challenged myself to keep working at improving. I had to overcome my stubbornness and the complacency developed from having negative tendencies for so long. One struggle I had with this process was a feeling that change was a bad thing because change had negative connotation in my life so far.

I developed confidence in my ability to make positive changes after I started making small improvements to my behavior. Interestingly, I discovered that these small steps of self-improvement worked together to improve my behavior more than I expected. The confidence I gained from small self-improvements fueled my determination to make further improvements and it became a snowball effect. I learned that no matter how confident I became or how many self-improvements I made, it was never enough because there were always more ways to improve. I did not lose confidence when I repeated the same stupid mistakes because I knew I would keep working at improving despite the setbacks.

I spent a lot of my time after school and during school breaks walking around my neighborhood and thinking. Walking up to houses and asking for work led to me helping with a garden, walking dogs, and mowing a yard for money. One day, I was walking through an elderly lady's yard when I stopped to ask her for work and started getting to know her. She was the kindest and most giving person I had ever known and I improved my behavior to fit in that environment. I was a much better person when I was around the elderly lady and did not want her to learn about all the negative things I was known for.

I never introduced the elderly lady to my family and I never told my second adoptive mom where I spent my time. I was put on probation for incorrigibility when I refused to tell my second adoptive mom where I went all day and refused to follow her directions in general. Being on probation did not stop me from spending time at the elderly lady's house or wandering around when I wanted. My behavior at home did not improve while I was on probation because I was too stubborn to let others see the good person I could be.

I waited until I moved to a new place to implement the self-improvements I had been working on for a while. Being guarded about myself was more important to me than being a better person even though I was secretly working on improving. I got the idea of starting with a blank slate when moving to a new place after I met the elderly lady while living at my second adoptive home. I figured out that I could use this method to implement my self-improvements without the embarrassment of letting other people know I was trying to be a better person. I started at a new school for seventh grade and took the opportunity to start with a blank slate but it did not work as intended.

I succeeded in implementing some self-improvements when I started seventh grade by not starting trouble, listening to teachers, and taking school work seriously. My self-improvements did not help because boys at school started bullying me daily and fighting back got me into trouble instead of them. I fought back against these boys every time and this just encouraged them because I was outnumbered and was not strong enough to beat them. The harassment got worse because the bullies learned they could get a reaction out of me and a group of boys even showed up at my house to harass me. I was stubborn about keeping different parts of my life separate, so I did not get my second adoptive mom involved with the harassment.

I finally got so fed up with the harassment that I made a threat against the kids to my second adoptive mom's boyfriend. I made the threat as a cry for help because I did not know how to express the intense anger I was feeling from being helpless. I did not know how to deal with this intense anger and fighting back against the bullies was just making the situation worse. This was not long after the infamous Columbine shooting and my second adoptive mom reported me to the school and police because she thought I might follow through with my threats. The school was not interested in punishing me, but making a threat while on probation landed me in the Juvenile Detention Center in LaPorte, Indiana three days before my fourteenth birthday.

CHAPTER THREE
The Centers

Ispent a little over a month at the Juvenile Detention Center and remained angry because I felt my situation was unfair. I had been the victim of bullying for months yet I was the one locked up while the despicable kids were probably out terrorizing a new victim. I was surprised that the kids I was locked up with were nicer to me than the kids getting away with bullying every day at my old school. I was momentarily discouraged because my attempts at self-improvement had not helped me in seventh grade, so I wondered if it was even worth the effort. This was the first place I met kids who obviously had harder lives than I did, which helped me start thinking about the struggles of others instead of just my own.

I went to court multiple times and the strip search I had anytime I left the building was embarrassing and seemed pointless since we were shackled and watched the entire time. My legal counsel recommended that I admit my threats were serious so I could get through this process faster and get out of the Juvenile Detention Center. I wanted to get back to my normal life as fast as I could so I lied to the judge and said the threats were serious. I could have explained the circumstances and told the truth, but I had no scruples about lying and was still guarded about myself. The judge determined I had not learned from my time at the Juvenile Detention Center and I did not seem to have remorse for my actions, so I was sent to another facility.

I left the Juvenile Detention Center and was placed at Midwest Center in Kouts, Indiana where I stayed about four months. One of the first staff members I met, tried to help put me at ease by putting the time I would spend at Midwest Center into perspective. He used a section of the wall to represent my life and a small segment within this section to represent the time I would be here. This did not help me because being at Midwest Center seemed like a big deal no matter how long I had to stay there. This mental picture did help later when I went through challenging times because I would remember this was just a small part of my overall life, so it was not a big deal.

Midwest Center had four units for troubled kids and I was placed in the one for boys in their early teens called the north unit. I got along with the staff and most of the other boys on the unit, so it was a pleasant experience for the most part. I ended up with a roommate with a lot of issues and he started being violent towards me when we were alone, so I started avoiding him whenever I could. There were certain points during the day when we had to stay in our rooms and I dreaded those times because I never knew if my roommate would decide to be violent. I was not believed when I accused my roommate of physical abuse because he was a sweet boy most of the time.

A staff member happened to walk by as my roommate was repeatedly punching me and the staff member intervened immediately. I was moved to a smaller unit meant for boys in their older teens, which was called the east unit. My time in the east unit made the bullying in seventh grade and my violent roommate from the north unit seem mild in comparison. My early days on the east unit were spent on my bed with my back to the wall and my knees up to protect my face from objects the boys would throw at me. These older boys were very good at being sneaky and some would even randomly walk in and punch me a couple times before walking out.

I did not trust the staff to protect me because no one had believed me when I reported abuse in seventh grade or on the north unit. I also feared the abuse would become worse if the boys caught me reporting their behavior, so I just endured through my time on the east unit. The boys on the east unit were older and tougher than anyone who had abused me previously, so I did not even try fighting back. I am not sure exactly what happened to finally get me moved from the east unit to the south unit. It is possible one of the boys on the unit let the staff know what was going on or the boys were not sneaky enough to get away with the abuse for long.

There was nowhere left for me to go since the north and east units were physically unsafe for me and the west unit was for girls in high school. My time on the south unit was much more enjoyable because only the best-behaved kids at Midwest Center were placed here and it was coed. The nicest staff chose to work on the south unit, so I was surrounded by some great adults and generally well-behaved kids. I had already been working on self-improvements and being surrounded by good examples motivated me to continue so I could fit in. This was the first point in my life where I realized I was truly making progress because people saw who I was now and could not believe I had been so bad before.

The consequence of the abuse I endured at Midwest Center made me become timid in stressful situations and a lot more withdrawn in general. I mentally conditioned myself to avoid risky situations and to try withdrawing when confrontations were initiated so I would not end up in similar situations again. I had grown up thinking I would fight back if any adults dared to abuse me, but my experiences at Midwest Center proved that notion to be false. Being abused at Midwest Center made me feel trapped and helpless to do anything about my situation, and I realized I would have had the same reaction if it had been adults in my life abusing me. My abuse lasted a couple months and I had to mentally adapt in irreversible ways so I could not imagine what long-term damage people had after years of abuse by adults in their life.

I left Midwest Center and spent the following year as a resident at Madison Center in South Bend, Indiana. Madison Center had blocks which were like the units for kids at Midwest Center and I was placed in the gamma block with boys in my age group. For the most part, the staff and other kids left me alone when I needed my space and were pleasant to be around. Some kids would pick on me from time to time, but this was a major improvement from the harassment and abuse I had experienced previously. My experiences and the environment at Madison Center were improvements compared to most of my time at previous placements.

Some of my biggest self-improvements were made at Madison Center because I had a lot of uninterrupted spare time to focus on self-reflection. One of the biggest improvements I made while at Madison Center was developing integrity because I lied constantly even when I gained nothing from it because it had developed into a habit. I made this major change so I would not have to juggle lies, and I would not have to stress about people finding out the truth. It was a challenge to myself to see if I could make such a drastic change. It was a challenge because the act of lying had become so natural that I did it without any effort so I had to be vigilant about catching myself before I lied. Becoming more honest caused me to improve my behavior in other ways so I would not self-incriminate myself with my determination to be honest.

It was during a family therapy session that my second adoptive mom explained why it would not be a good idea for me to go back to live with her. She explained that the environment at home had not improved, so she worried it would not do me any good to come back because there was a risk of me continuing my destructive behaviors. This meant I had no home or family anymore, so I did not get weekend passes to leave even though my behavior always earned me passes for the whole weekend. I tried to convince myself everything was fine and I did not need anyone, but this did not stop me from losing hope about my future and becoming depressed.

My intense feelings of depression were directed internally where I wallowed in the misery while my intense anger had been directed externally where it affected others. My intense feelings shifting from anger to depression could be likened to a blazing star becoming a black hole. Depression was having a negative impact on my life so I let a doctor prescribe medication for me after I accepted I could not handle depression on my own. Sometimes, I stopped taking my medication through the years because I thought I did not need it anymore or was not able to buy more so I would slowly lose motivation. A vicious cycle occurred when I knew my depression was getting worse, but lacked the motivation to improve my situation, so the depression and lack of motivation would spiral out of control.

CHAPTER FOUR
High School

I started taking freshman classes while I was at Madison Center because I took a test which showed I was advanced enough to be moved up from eighth grade. I switched schools too often during my first year of high school to earn any credits and I even had to go over material like Romeo and Juliet at three different schools. I attended John Adams High School in South Bend, Indiana for half days while living at Madison Center because my good behavior earned me the privilege. I ended my first year of high school at Whites in Wabash, Indiana and was told I would have to redo the entire freshman year since I had not earned any credits yet. I was angry about putting effort into learning and having it amount to nothing just because progress at different schools was not coordinated.

I left Madison Center in April and was transferred to Whites, which is a facility located in Wabash, Indiana. My placement at Whites was a reward for my great behavior at Madison Center since Whites had more freedom for residents such as not having to be supervised by adults as much. Whites was meant to be a temporary placement while a foster home was found for me since I had nowhere to live. I tried to explain the circumstances that resulted in my transfer to Whites, but my story was too unbelievable since Whites is not a facility meant for well-behaved kids. The communication for my transfer to Whites was so abysmal that I was placed with the worst kids at Whites despite my great behavior that got me sent there.

I resigned myself to the fact I would be at Whites longer than I first expected since the staff disregarded what I told them about my behavior at Madison Center and the judge's directive to find me a foster home. I made the most of my time at Whites by taking advantage of opportunities such as working in the cafeteria where I helped serve food and washed dishes. I had problems with other kids in my assigned house at Whites, but I tried avoiding conflicts by being friendly with everyone so the problems did not escalate into anything serious. I felt vindicated when the judge asked about the progress in finding me a foster home and the staff member who took me had no response since they did not know about it. I felt like screaming, "I told you so" to all the people who had not believed me, but I had too much self-control and it would not have helped the situation anyway.

I learned from my time at Whites that even unfortunate events such as being placed with the worst kids, could turn out to have a positive impact on my life. It was because of my house placement at Whites that I met a foster lady who went out of her way to help me on numerous occasions. She was the foster parent of one of the other residents in my house at Whites, and she started getting to know me when she found out I had no one to visit me and nowhere to go for weekend passes. The foster lady would send me care packages, brought me treats when she visited her foster son, and gave me the feeling of hope and someone caring about me which I was lacking. I remained in contact with her until the present time and even became best friends with one of her other foster kids.

There was a staff member at Whites who already had a foster son about my age, so I had a trial visit with his family to see if I would be a good fit. I moved to Walton, Indiana in September to live with my third foster family after they decided I would do well in their home. Walton was a small farming town with a population of about one thousand people where my third foster family rented a house surrounded by corn fields. I enjoyed the peacefulness of being in the middle of nowhere after living in facilities for the previous two years. The best part of living at my third foster home was meeting my foster brother who I kept in contact with long after leaving foster care because we had a lot in common.

I became obsessed with a new trading

card game while living with my third foster family, and I resorted to stealing cards from stores since I did not have the money to feed my addiction. I had not learned my lesson from the last time I got addicted to a trading card game and spent a lot of time thinking of strategies and competing against anyone I could. I eventually figured out I was susceptible to becoming addicted so I started avoiding anything I might get addicted to such as smoking, alcohol, or drugs. I had various people through the years assume my parents were in jail for drugs and this stopped me from using these substances so I would not end up like that. The negative feelings I associated with these substances did not go away even after I found out the speculations about my parents were not true.

I finished my second year as a freshman while living with my third foster family and earned all my credits this time through. I was not able to stay with my third foster family because my foster dad was offered a teaching job in Tennessee and he did not want to pass up the opportunity. I was asked where I wanted to live and I chose Michigan

City, Indiana so I could see my old friend from elementary school. I was told the closest foster home to Michigan City was a family in Portage, Indiana so I chose them in the hopes I could still visit my friend occasionally. This was the first time my input was considered for where I was going to live and it felt good having some control.

I went to live with my fourth foster family and spent my sophomore and junior years of high school there. My fourth foster family was originally from Canada and had also lived in the Middle East, so they had a lot of interesting experiences to tell me about. The money from taking in foster kids was helpful in supplementing my foster dad's unemployment checks since he had lost his good-paying job in Chicago, Illinois. My fourth foster parents were great examples of hard workers because they were oftentimes busy volunteering at food banks, doing projects for their church, chopping wood for their wood stove, or working on the garden that took up the entire back yard. My foster dad was inspiring to me because he did not let the struggles in his life such as type 1 diabetes, stop him from accomplishing his goals and being productive.

Meeting my biological family was made possible when the foster lady I met at Whites used her resources to help me accomplish this goal. No one involved with my case had any idea how to help me find my family even though the judge had given a directive for them to try. My fourth foster family allowed me to stay with them to finish my junior year even though I turned eighteen and was reunited with my biological family before the school year was over. Being allowed to stay at the same school the whole school year provided the stability that helped me stay focused on completing my goal of graduating. I spent the holidays with my biological family in Fort Wayne, Indiana, which gave me the opportunity to meet and get to know more of my family members.

A consequence of staying with my fourth foster family was not getting to know my biological grandfather as much as I wanted before he passed away. My maternal grandfather was one of my family members who I had strong bonds with before going into foster care, so it was quite painful when he died four months after I was reunited with him. The best memory I have of my grandfather was during Christmas break when he drove my youngest biological sister and I to visit one of my aunts in North Carolina. My grandfather was one of the most selfless people I have ever met and his example influenced me to work even harder on my self-improvements. I attended his funeral in March and moved back to Fort Wayne to live with my biological family the following June.

My emotions were intense from my long-awaited reunion and I started comparing my biological family to the perfect picture I had developed over the years in my imagination. Reality did not come close to matching my unrealistic expectations, so my emotions were all over the place while I tried to adapt to my new environment. My intense feelings caused me to overreact, so I would isolate myself and listen to music for hours until I could get my feelings under control again. Listening to music helped me regulate my feelings because I would start by listening to music that matched my mood before listening to gradually calmer music until

I was calm myself. I used the technique of listening to music enough times that I internalized the process and did not need to work as hard at regulating my feelings.

I wanted a reunion with my oldest biological sister more than anything and I remembered my first adoptive parents' names so I just needed the courage to contact her. I searched the internet to make a list of anyone in Indiana with the same first and last names of my first adoptive parents, then started calling all of them to ask if my sister was there. I was successful in my search and started getting to know my sister over the phone and on messenger until she started avoiding contact with me. She asked me not to give her contact information to anyone in our biological family so I did not and I respected her decision when it became clear she did not want contact with me either. I thought about contacting her over the years to see if she changed her mind about getting to know her biological family, but I decided against it each time since she already made her decision clear.

I came to accept my sister's decision to not have contact with her biological family after I put myself in her situation. I realized she entered foster care and was adopted at such a young age, so her current family is the only one she had created bonds with. I also might not have had a desire to reunite with my biological family if I had not built strong bonds with them in the time before entering foster care. It sounded like she had a very loving and supportive family so there was no reason to risk the complications of trying to incorporate two different families into her life. I eventually came to accept the picture-perfect reunion I envisioned while growing up was not going to happen.

I spent my senior year at North Side High School at the same time my youngest sister was a freshman there. I decided to challenge myself by taking all the honors classes I could, just to prove to myself I could do well even though I had never tried one before my senior year. Being in honors classes helped because I was surrounded by motivated and well-behaved students who had no interest in distracting me from my goal of graduating. I had always wondered how I would have turned out if I never went into foster care, so I pushed myself to be my best even though I could never recreate who I would have been. I graduated midyear at the age of nineteen and did well enough on my SAT test to be accepted into a local college.

CHAPTER FIVE
College

I chose to attend Indiana University-Purdue University Fort Wayne (IPFW) because it had a department of anthropology and was close to where I lived. My biological mother allowed me to stay with her and my youngest biological sister while I worked towards my degree in anthropology. I chose anthropology because it had fascinated me since fourth grade, and I did not take the career prospects into as much consideration as I should have. College was a lot more enjoyable than primary and secondary school because I was in control of which classes I took within the confines of the bingo sheet I needed for graduation. The stress of college and working as a third shift stocker was too much for me so I chose to focus on my school responsibilities because my grades were suffering from being overwhelmed.

I was in IPFW's library one day when I met a girl I was interested in getting to know better. We were attracted to each other, but her religion did not allow her to date people from outside their church. I spent over a year waiting patiently for the girl from IPFW to leave her church like she planned since it was such a controlling environment. The fulfillment I felt from helping this girl overcome her tendency to rely on others to make decisions for her made it clear I should be doing something with my life that involved helping people. One major problem we had was she wanted to always keep me happy because she was a people pleaser, but my feelings were far too intense for her to influence them without a lot of effort.

We drifted apart over time and the feeling of betrayal when we parted ways was quite intense considering we were never in a committed relationship. This betrayal I felt was compounded by all the other hurt that had been building up over the years and I broke down for several months. My depression was so intense that I could not function properly which led to me sleeping most of the day and barely getting out of bed even when I was awake. Nothing mattered to me because all I focused on was all the misery in my life which felt like a never-ending list. I flunked all the classes I was taking since I stopped attending which led to my funding being withdrawn and I could not return due to the debt I now owed the school.

I worked through my feeling enough to not be crippled by the depression and accepted I could no longer battle depression on my own. I got some professional help and the medication they prescribed helped me feel motivated enough to start caring about what happened with my life. I was not able to return to college so I worked at a grocery store down the road as a cashier and cleaner. It did not take long for me to realize I wanted more out of my life and I was not going to help people in a meaningful way through this job. I knew that I wanted a job that would challenge me to keep improving, and this job was not going to fulfill that desire so I did not feel too bad when I lost the job.

My paternal grandfather was gracious enough to help me learn to drive and I went driving with him occasionally. It was during one of these driving lessons when I was parking in front of a tree and stepped on the gas pedal instead of the brake pedal and ended up putting a crack in his windshield. My grandfather did not make a big deal out of the damage and still wanted to help me, so he paid for a driving class. I was eager to prove I could get my license despite my anxiety, so I followed through with the class and obtained my driver's license. That was as far as my determination to overcome my intense driving anxiety went because I only tried driving one more time in the next nine years.

I eventually narrowed my options for a career down to social work, therapy, or teaching at the elementary level since my past experiences could have been useful in any of these career paths. There were negative connotations I had developed towards social workers and therapists which grew from me thinking they could not adequately understand my circumstances enough to help. Social workers and therapists were directly connected to challenging times in my life so these two careers could have been an unwanted reminder of my past. I wanted to blend in with others the best I could, so having this constant reminder that I needed these services myself for years was not something that was going to help my internal façade. There was always the fear that I would regret my career decision later in life no matter how much thought I put into it before committing.

After months of deliberation, I chose to pursue a bachelor's degree in elementary education because I wanted a career focused on helping people and enjoyed working with kids. A lot of professors wanted to know the reasoning behind students choosing teaching as a profession to make sure students were going in with good intentions and not just wanting long summer breaks. I knew on the inside that I wanted to potentially help kids who might be going through their own struggles but outwardly I did not want to divulge my past. This was normal for me because I did not want to be treated any differently or risk people feeling pity for me. I also hoped my deep thinking would help me break difficult concepts into smaller parts that would be easier for students to understand.

I attended a church with my paternal grandparents where I met a man who was interested in helping me get back into college. I explained how my debt to the college was stopping me from continuing my education and how I would go back if I could. The man from church proceeded to help me pay off my debt by giving me various jobs at his house. The man from church helped me graduate college by giving me encouragement when the stress of college felt like it was going to overwhelm me. I knew that I did not want my life to go to waste and thankfully it did not because of his assistance and my determination to use what I learned from my past to benefit others.

I stopped going to church periodically because I wanted to take time to think about ideas more deeply before I trusted what the churches were teaching. I struggled with the concept of a God who is good and all-powerful yet still allowed evil and suffering like what others and I had gone through. Being omniscient meant God already knew whether people would end up in Heaven or Hell so I did not understand the charade of having people live through their Earthly existence. I wondered why Hell existed when God loved His creations and wanted them to choose eternity with Him yet created a place for some of his creations to suffer for eternity. These aspects of religion did not make sense, but having a God who created the laws of the universe and everything in it was easier to accept than a big bang originating from nothing.

I put so much time and effort thinking about religion because I did not know what to believe after learning different religious viewpoints from each family I lived with. I was not able to take the easy path and base my faith on my family's beliefs since I did not have just one family growing up. This led me to spend a lot of time thinking about the same concepts except from different viewpoints to figure out which perspective made the most sense to me. My conclusions focused on the dichotomy of good and evil and how both were necessary for free will to be possible. This meant the need for Jesus to be sent as a sacrifice to have imperfect creations have free will and still have an opportunity to spend an eternity with God.

I spent a lot of my free time playing an online game during high school and college. This online game was appealing because it had no level or skill caps so I could improve my character as much as I wanted. There was a parallel between my in-game and my real-life character because both had goals for improvement that I kept extending when I reached them. I used this online game as an escape from the overwhelming world around me in the same way I used to play trading card games and read books when I was younger. The benefit of obsessing and immersing myself into games and books was not being stressed about the world around me because my attention was focused on these escape mechanisms.

I felt such a sensation of peace when escaping the stressful world around me that I did not think about the negative consequences. I kept trying to justify my time playing this online game by thinking if I enjoyed wasting the time, then it was not really wasted. This was a dangerous way of thinking because my obsession distracted me from other important parts of my life. I finally accepted that I would not have time for my obsessions if I wanted to do my best as a teacher because I knew it was going to be a time-consuming job. I ended up selling my account to pay for tests I needed to become a licensed teacher, and I knew I would not return to the game after losing the thousands of hours I put into that game character.

CHAPTER SIX
Teaching

I spent the summer after graduation unsuccessfully searching for a teaching position in the Fort Wayne area. This was unfortunate because I thought having my own classroom would make the hard work I put into graduating college worthwhile. I wanted my own classroom so I could have a better chance of making a difference in kids' lives since I would have a full year to help them. I also did not want to be a substitute teacher my first year because I wanted a better paying job to help pay off my student loans. I was determined to have my own classroom, so I looked for areas with teacher shortages since there was none where I lived.

I searched online and saw the Las Vegas school system needed teachers because of high turnover. I figured it was worth my time to apply since I would have an easier time getting a job in a school system with a shortage. I was guaranteed a job, but was nervous when I saw claims of applicants being blacklisted when they turned down a job offer from the first principal interviewing them. The principal who interviewed me warned that he expected me to have the effectiveness of a third-year teacher by the end of my first year. I was excited to get a teaching job and loved a challenge, so I was okay with these extreme expectations.

The man from church who helped me get back into college offered to help me move to Las Vegas, so I accepted the fourth-grade position over the phone. He thought the job was a good career and learning opportunity because the school had improved a lot because of the principal's guidance. His assistance and faith in me went above and beyond anything I expected. His financial help included a plane ticket, food to last until I had my first paycheck, furniture, household essentials, and even the first month's rent. The money was a loan and he asked me to pass on the goodwill by helping someone else like he had helped me.

I was excited about my move to Las Vegas because it was different than all the other times I had moved. I did not know anyone who lived in Las Vegas when I moved there and was living on my own. This meant I did not have to stress about adjusting to fit in like I did when I moved into a new foster home. I tried even harder to have a good start to my career because I did not want to let my friend from church down after he helped so much. Having this stressful job hurt my attempts at making connections since I was usually overwhelmed and did not have much spare time.

SPS had a bigger impact on my teaching than I expected when administrators came into the classroom to observe my teaching. The nervousness and pressure I felt was overwhelming because I knew these observations were determining if I would have a job the following year. I could not stop thinking about what conclusions the administrator might be forming based on every little aspect of my teaching or students' behavior. I was afraid my mind would shut down to protect itself if I tried to process everything, so I focused on the lesson I was teaching during observations. Having off task students made me look bad, but having a nervous breakdown would have been worse. I would go home after school and work through my nervousness from the observation because I was rattled the rest of the day.

The worst behaving students in fourth grade had been split between two master teachers since there were going to be two new fourth-grade teachers joining the school. I replaced one of these master teachers when she got promoted to a teaching coach position, but the class lists were not altered to reflect this change. There was a lot going on with many new teachers and expectations were high from the school, so class lists were overlooked. As a first-year teacher, I struggled to handle a class intended for a veteran teacher who had mastered classroom management long ago. It was a third-grade teacher who figured out why I had been struggling so much all year, but it was too far into the school year to shuffle kids around.

My fourth-grade class was made up of thirty students, and ten of them were so disruptive and disrespectful that the learning of everyone was negatively impacted. I would come to school a couple hours early each school day to get everything ready and mentally prepare myself for the day ahead. It did not matter that I started each day with optimism for change and prepared myself because the reality of failing at making progress left me discouraged when the students went home. Administrators were extremely busy, so they did not discipline my students appropriately and were not able to provide the support I needed to make an effective learning environment. I kept trying to teach my students empathy by explaining how their behavior was negatively affecting the other students, but my efforts were ineffective so it didn't improve their behavior.

My teaching contract was not renewed for the next school year so I moved back to Fort Wayne with my biological mother. I was disappointed in myself for my failure as a teacher in Las Vegas, so I did not have a lot of enthusiasm while I searched for a teaching job with Fort Wayne Community Schools. The black mark from my failed year of teaching hurt my chances of getting my own classroom, so I did not have much hope against the surplus of potential teachers. I went through the process of becoming a substitute teacher when it was obvious I would not get a classroom of my own. There were no career options I could think of for helping people as much as a teacher could, and I did not want my license as a teacher to be wasted so I spent the next three years as a substitute teacher.

I had a pattern as a teacher that I never figured out how to break because I treated students how I would want to be treated which led to me failing as a teacher every time. I was extremely flexible and tried my best to be understanding and show compassion towards students because I wanted them to feel comfortable with being their true selves around me. I developed this knack for getting people to be themselves around me because I refrained from judging others after all the horrible things I did. One benefit of students opening up to me was learning their honest opinions on many topics without them worrying about me judging them for it. Disrespectful students showing their inner selves during class, resulted in disruptive behavior. I never found a way to effectively explain how it was only acceptable to be themselves when it did not interfere with the learning of their peers.

Disruptive behaviors would spiral out of control and disrespect was aimed at me when I reprimanded these same students who I had been compassionate and understanding with before. This led to students perceiving me as mean because I would not tolerate these behaviors when they were interrupting class. The backlash of disrespect due to me being perceived as mean would spiral out of control over time. I knew that I needed to be consistent from the beginning so this cycle would not repeat yet I was never successful in doing so. I never managed to achieve a balance between being overly compassionate versus being overly strict. Giving all this attention to disruptive students was a disservice to those students who wanted to learn, so I would move on when it was apparent that the problem would not be fixed.

My teaching philosophy was derived from what my own teachers did during my time in school. I did not find it strange when my teachers let students sleep, play card games in class, or read off-topic books. The idea of students being responsible for their own learning stuck with me beyond my time as a teacher and I agreed with it wholeheartedly. My realization that teaching was not a feasible career due to frustration of my shortcomings and lack of improvement in the school system developed steadily over these four years. Yet, I had seen all the improvement accomplished in my life when some may have seen no hope. This helped me hold out hope that I could help people even if it was through writing a book instead of traditional teaching.

CHAPTER SEVEN
Eighth Family

I was determined to prove to myself that I could still be useful to others especially after feeling like such a failure for struggling during my first year of teaching. This led me to help people when I normally would have declined because I usually did not want to be overwhelmed by other people's problems when I had enough of my own. I was visiting my best friend, who I met when he was in foster care with the lady I met at Whites, when I was given an opportunity to be useful to someone. My best friend's sister-in-law was stressed out about her daughter's sweet sixteen party and asked if I would replace someone who dropped out. I agreed to help with the party even though helping meant I would be included in a dance routine in front of party guests.

I disliked dancing and being in front of others, so I had a lot of anxiety as I helped setup the decorations for the party. Something amazing happened that day when I met the girl who would eventually become my life companion and help me raise our daughter. I had almost given up on ever finding someone who could handle being with someone with my baggage so I had my doubts alongside my reluctance to form new bonds. Our fortuitous relationship was thankfully not marred by my RAD because this part of me has focused on protecting me from harmful separations rather than isolating me from relationships altogether. I enjoyed the transition from a life focused on myself to one focused on my new family because my life felt somewhat empty beforehand even though I had devoted my life to helping others through my career.

Being a father was challenging because my parenting ideas were influenced by many sources including what I learned about children's development in college. I was scared I would not be a great father given that I had grown up without a consistent father figure. For most my childhood, I did not have a father figure so I looked up the benefits of a father being an active part of a child's life to feel reassured that my role was important. I made building a strong relationship with my daughter a priority and it went well, so I gradually stopped doubting my ability to help provide a loving environment for her to grow up in. I was determined not to let my daughter develop the trust issues I have, so it was a priority for her to know she could trust the caretakers in her life.

I had an inner turmoil over the years about whether the apathy from RAD or the compassion from SPS was my real foundation within. It came down to wondering if I was an apathetic person pretending to myself and the world that I was compassionate or the other way around. This contradiction led me to lengths of time trying to focus on the apathy or the compassion within, so I could figure this conundrum out. It did not matter how many times over the years I switched back and forth because it always seemed like there was a part of me missing. It was not until I accepted the influences of RAD and SPS were equally a part of who I was before the balance between these aspects of myself could occur.

It had been many years since I needed the mental protections obtained through distancing myself, yet RAD never stopped influencing me. RAD kept me more distanced than I would have liked and probably led me to not make the connections with people which could have allowed me to help better. I could be as compassionate as others who focused on empathy, yet I could also instantly go from caring about a person and not caring about their existence like flipping a switch. This probably stemmed from needing to make this type of drastic change early in life towards entire families, but it was still disconcerting to experience this abrupt apathy for people I cared about. This abrupt switching between caring and apathy usually happened when I was having major problems with someone, so it was thankfully a rare occurrence and was as quickly undone when the person wanted reconciliation with me.

I ended my career as a teacher without a clear path laid out for my future. My plan was to help people along the lines of social work or something similar that would allow me to positively impact the lives of others. My focus turned to finishing a book about how foster care, facilities, being adopted twice, and how RAD and SPS impacted my life. I had been going back and forth about whether a book about my life would benefit others since high school. I had the title and an outline for the book for many years, so I just had to convince myself of the merits of publishing something that many people probably could not relate to. What finally convinced me to go through with finishing the book was thinking of the millions of people it could help instead of the hundreds of millions it would not interest.

Made in the USA
Lexington, KY
25 July 2017